WHAT FLIES AWAY

WHAT FLIES AWAY

POEMS

STACY DONEY

Illustrated by

AMBER JACKOLA

Tiushe Publishing

Library of Congress Control Number 2022920624

Paperback ISBN 978-1-954175-82-2
Electronic ISBN 978-1-954175-83-9

Distributed by Tivshe Publishing
Printed in the United States of America

Cover design and interior artwork by Amber Jackola

Visit www.tivshepublishing.com

CONTENTS

For Mrs. Fuchs

STORGÉ

Second child, weary with schoolwork
crawls into my arms, quiet, still.
No sleep, no words,
just a reunion of heart rhythm.

NON-ATTACHMENT

One day I stopped fighting for a just life.
In between confidence and doubt
is the flight of pure experience:
a heart that expands in all directions
and lets before and after
fly up like embers.

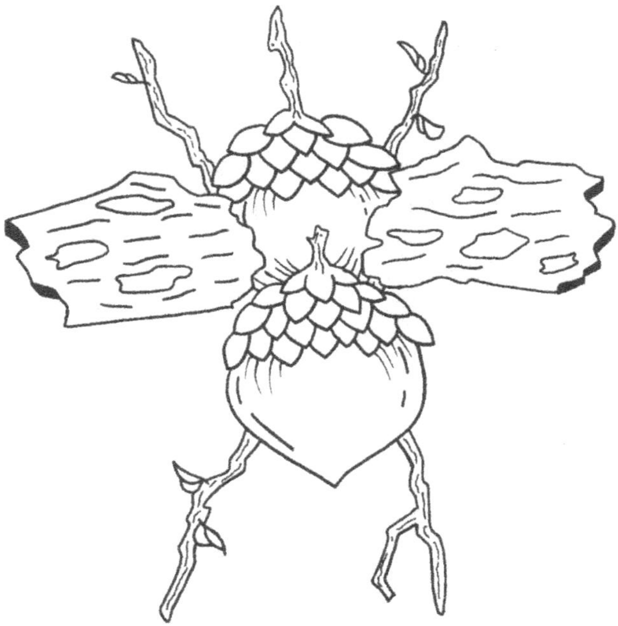

THE TOYMAKER

In my shop, painted, wooden, beetles
are lined up like matchbox cars.
I've carved them from a fallen red oak,
and I'm proud of their sturdy forms,
though I know time will leave them scratched and
    faded.

I'm looking forward to the winter Solstice
and the gift-giving time,
and afterwards,
the tucked-in, wind-swept days
of quiet idleness.
I'm yearning for muffled afternoons
of snow, hot tea,
and the children and I sprawled on the floor.
The wooden beetles will glitter in our hands
as we narrate a summer story to give them life.

A long time ago,
the master toy maker told me,
Never scold a child over a broken toy.

The gift is not in the toy.
It is in the playing.

And now, as I carve and paint,
slowing my breath to steady my hand,
a smile softens through me.

The work of play will wear away forms and colors,
leaving signs of all the time we've spent breathing
    together,
touching toy to toy, bumping hands,
nudging shoulders, whispering, laughing.
We'll trace a map of memories on each wooden toy.

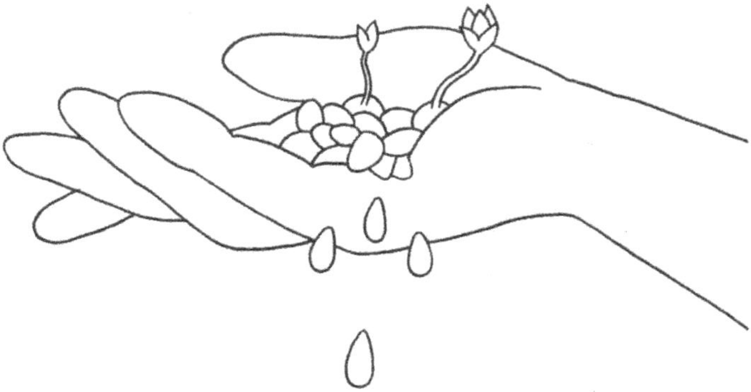

WAITING FOR FLOWERS

On the news they're saying,
Twelve years until the point of no return,
and now I'm floating away from everything,
almost forty years in the past,
inside Fox Memorial Hospital.
It's the point of no return for my grandmother.
She knows it, and so do I.
Words don't serve well at such times.
A heart frozen in fear speaks without substance or not
at all.

I'm coming back down to earth now,
blowing warm air into my hands,
holding them over my heart.
Now I'm pulling them away,
and they're full of seeds.
If I've got the math right,
twelve years is twelve springs,
twelve summers,
twelve planting seasons.
Maybe twelve hundred flower seeds

could drop from these hands.

No flower goes back in the seed.
No human goes back in the womb.
Life is not built for return.
When conditions are right,
new seeds germinate.
Let me put my faith in that.

LATE FEBRUARY

Red foxes cry out to one another under the new
moon.
I push up the window to hear them better.
The darkness makes me strain my ears to follow their
pacing pathways.
Broad silence is punctuated with their sharp, rasping,
screams.
Loping through the naked blueberry bushes,
weaving through the oaks and black gum trees,
their voices travel uphill,
until the cat is pacing in wide circles through the
house.
When dog and vixen find each other,
the heat of their red-flanked bodies
will rise to the tops of the red maples.
Only weeks from now,
the sky will blush crimson with flowers,
as if remembering this lusty night.

SKY-LIKE MIND

Evening darkens down
over the garden and surrounding trees.
There's no moon,
only gray sky, flecked with mica.

A wood thrush
sings out like a piccolo,
all swirling notes
and staccato buzz

rising over the percussion of a distant train.
My heart and lungs
work faster to keep pace with the song.
My breath draws in

the spice of leaf litter and mycelium.
Now I'm a song, a wheel, a distant star,
no separation between us,
all of us in one great turning.

WALKING MEDITATION

I'm standing with my eyes closed,
waiting for the bell.
I feel into the acute angle of my body,
wider at the base.

At the sharp, full, sound of the bell,
I open my eyes,
breath in, and take slow steps,
across the tender moss.

Each time I turn to walk back again,
I stop shy of a hole the size of a black walnut
that could be for a snake, a vole, or a mouse,
but I hope, for a snake.

A dark hole is not always a source of danger.
A dark place in the heart
does not have to cause fear.
Walking towards darkness and away again

with slow steps and slow breaths,
I am friends with myself again.
This slow walk back to wholeness
that goes nowhere and everywhere at once.

HIGH TEA

When the tulip tree blooms,
I long to drink from those green and gold cups
ringed with fire.

Tea is served only to the sky,
who drops the cups to the ground
a fortnight later.

In the morning, before I'm awake,
bandit ants break them apart further,
until no last sip is left.

I hunt between crowded
blueberry bushes,
hoping to find one still whole.

But all are ruined,
and a mocking squirrel jester
laughs and shouts,
too, too, too laaaaaate!

EEK-OLOGY

The cicadas zip through sun-streamed treetops,
wild from their seventeen-year wait.
They veer into our windshield,
and the smack
jerks us back.
For a moment we mourn their poor luck.
Such dedicated stillness
ending
in a belly flop.

REST LAYING DOWN WITH MOTION

The weight of her body is molded to my chest.
A sudden agitation of limbs,
and she sighs and turns her head back and forth.
It comes down hard on my breastbone each time,
just over my heart,
a beat straining to be met
by a steadier one.

I lay as still as dried moss.
She is a thrum of life and will,
wanting to sink down
like rainwater in good soil.
I'm here with her while she does the
work of letting go.

When sleep is at last
breathing through her,
like wind through pine needles,
I move out from under her,
place a hand on her little back,

just for a moment,
to seal the spell of sleep,
and slip away.

TWO BIRDS

I walk barefoot over moss, clover, and grass,
my bones grinding louder than my thoughts,
my thoughts a heavy pack of worries.

Over my left shoulder
comes a flutter of feathers and song,
and two birds glide past me into the high oak ahead.
My back lengthens and I rise to my toes,

smiling.
I breath in the same air
that lifted their wings a moment ago,
and all worry is gone.

In my heart,
a bird spreads her wings
in a wide wave,
while another bird looks on.

I am the one who worries
and the one who smiles

and the one who watches
from the high oak of my mind.

I am the flight and the moment before flight
and the action that turns stillness to flight.
I am the flight bones and the hollows within them.
I am the empty air and the currents of air.

I am the one who was lost.
I am the one now found
and the one who will lead her astray again.

Walk out the door,
see if you can find me
before you lose the memory
of what you were looking for.

INATTENTION

I'm pulling down maple and black gum branches,
pruning them mindlessly,
making a clear path for my husband
and the red lawn mower.
Another aggressive yank
and I see fast, black, yellow,
circling, hornets
meeting my attention with their own.
A red welt rises on my arm
and a heat that teaches me
my place.

HUNGRY GHOSTS

hungry ghosts fill every space between us in this realm and suck the air from around us with their tiny mouths they would cry if they could open their jaws but there's no way to unhinge them further instead they unhinge us and confuse our speech until we feed them with the words of loss

WHAT FLIES AWAY

a wood thrush beats against window glass
my finger becomes a branch
to carry her outside

loss is a child's hand pointing
at what flies away
as all things do

a gold moth scooped from the pool
unfolds and is gone
my hand still wet

loss is a child's hand pointing
at what flies away
as all things do

my daughter enters
her friend's house on our old block
where the maple we planted is dying

loss is a child's hand pointing
at what flies away
as all things do

idling at the curb
watching my son walk to the dorm
the rearview mirror too small

loss is a child's hand pointing
at what flies away
as all things do

after the storm
my husband stands by a fallen oak
that natural smile fallen too.

loss is a child's hand pointing
at what flies away
as all things do

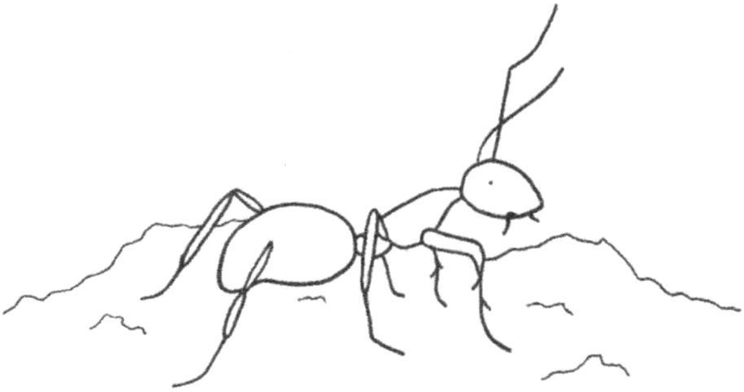

WHERE WE'RE GOING

The angel of this place
will one summer at a time
allow the trees
and the ants
to overtake this house.
Green and black
will spread in fractals
inside and outside our walls.

Backyard serenades by cicadas
lull us into believing
we're a part of it all.
But we can't help imagining
Cutting down the trees and
poisoning the ants
if they get too close.

Green and black
and the angel of this place
live in every crack
of every wall

and the elements
adore them.
We're not sure if we're good
or useful
and secretly suspect the angel
of ignoring us.

The trees stare straight into the sun.
The ants see through the walls.
We wear glasses
just to see
where we're going,
and yet
we still don't know.

MIRROR NEURONS

Your voice jumps pitch,
higher, tighter,
coming
out
in
pops.
My heart rate
picks
up
The
beat
and matches it,
marching me down
a rocky,
dirt,
road
too fast for reason or safety

until I reach out for a tree limb
to steady myself
and draw in my breath

slowly,
then send it out
and down,
like December's last oak leaves

falling,
then
floating
in spiral
curves
back
to earth.

If I could care for this breath
more than these troublesome thoughts
peace would reign in my life
forever.

PERMISSION TO YELL

You're doing it again.
This body is bone and muscle,
no gears.

It's not okay to never rest.
Unlock your jaw.
Tell them,
Give me ten minutes!

And watch them scatter
like ants
after the rock is pulled away.

HEART MAGIC

Paper hearts fall
from the branches of the redbud tree every autumn,
yet the roots hold steady until spring.
Lavender pink flowers will one morning
crown the branches
drawing my eye and deepening my breath.

In this dry season
I wipe away the dust on my table.
I call it "the dust."
I call the table "mine."
The table is not from me,
but the dust is.
Yet I love the table more.

I've seen a fallen pine
become dust over a span of years.
In the springtime purple violets and bellwort
grow a short distance away.
I can't stop longing for them
even though I know they'll return.

I'll go down on my knees
to the leathery leaves and damp earth.
My begging hand will lift flowers to see inside.
It will be the gateway to my own heart
and the strengthening of my blood.

I want to root myself deeper,
trusting this earth
and my place in her cycles,
even when all seems dying around me.

The elemental magic
of one thing becoming another
is the spell that dry leaves whisper
on the way down.

STRONG ENOUGH

This new kitten
keeps her eyes full as ant hills
and every sound
twists her ears around
like those ants searching,
squaring space rapidly,
looking, smelling.

Her cool nose taps mine.
Her eyes are as wide as a
wanting heart.
She wants the smell of Mother
but gets the scent of coffee and oatmeal instead.

My arms are stronger than her,
and I carry her to bed,
but her paws still
push away
like a spider hurtling fast
from a web I broke through.

I've arranged the walk-in closet
with pillows, blankets, and her cat bed,
and lay down next to her each night.

In the quietest part of the house,
her purring soothes us both.
I wonder if weakness or strength
makes me stay with her while she falls asleep.

I'm strong enough,
but both a kitten and a spider
can bring me to my knees.

It took some years living in the woods
to be gentle with the spiders.
I know some of them now.

Like the castleback orbweaver
that dangled from my arm yesterday,
deposited on a blueberry bush
with an apology from me,
Sorry about your web.

There is a way of strength only possible
without rushing.
A way of reaching out,
holding on,
holding still.

To unhook from a claw,
yield and move closer.
To break away from a web,
stop and step back.
Using your strength to save all beings,
you will also save yourself.

STARFLOWERS

Autumn is the season of goldenrod and aster.
Little stars among the grasses light up the landscape.
Dusk comes early now,
but their brilliance is found even in moonlight.

Walking back inside,
even if I close my eyes, I can still see them.

In September, I left the house for a walk,
my thoughts crowded with the endless harms
that penetrate our lives,
like slugs on bee balm.

What's the point of anything, I thought.
My forehead tight, I looked up.

Four or five aster blooms were newly open,
the eyes of morning
looking into my own.
Nothing had changed in my life but this,

and still,
I smiled.

NO SELF

Tulip tree seeds click in wild swirls over the patio.
So many thousands and only two mother trees in the
woods,
one north, one south of the house.
Some fall still stacked together
in rings like papal tiaras.

Once I found a forked twig
with a cone on either side.
I keep it in a box still,
and sometimes admire its ridged bark,
an open cone on one side, a closed cone on the other.

The open cone is fringed
like the tube I lost to the surgeon's knife
at thirty-five (The rest cut out at forty-two).
I have the photographs in a filing cabinet.

They are of rounded forms,
glistening red, pink, white and grey,
pulled aside by steel instruments.

Looking at them makes me hold my breath.

At times I thought I hadn't said a proper goodbye
to those parts of myself.
All while carelessly scrubbing skin cells away,
tossing my own hair into the trash,
and releasing waste almost hourly.

Now I watch how much a tulip tree loses,
while she tells me,
all goes back to the earth, whether by wind, blade, or
gravity.
Each time my fingers dig into damp soil,
I try to remember this.

SILENT RETREAT

I'm standing alone in the kitchen,
amazed that you got on the bus today.
I was so sure you'd try to stay home.
The noise, the cliques, the crowds,
the throbbing in your forehead.
But you went,
and without a word between us.

Last night at dinner,
I'd felt a tension in me,
wanting reassurance that you'd go.
But I said nothing.

I'd been reading about silent retreats,
and wondered if I could be silent
about even one subject.
The fantasy of a week in the mountains,
without responsibilities,
was fading
along with any confidence
that I could let go of worry

for even one cycle of breath.

This morning you hugged me goodbye
at the backdoor,
your hair cool and scented with rose shampoo.
You hurried out, silent as a moth.

I stayed still as an empty cocoon,
watching from the window,
and having no answer as to how you did it,
my mind was, at last, empty.

OLDEST CHILD BAKING

When you fell to the floor
In tears, chest heaving,
I realized how alone
you were,
even with my hand soft on your back.

Two cakes promised to your
French class.
This one is ragged.
The next one will be better,
after you follow my advice
and circle the pan with the
cake knife.

But I'll always believe
the first cake was best,
because it showed me again
how deep the well of your heart is
and how sweet the water.

GRADUATION

All walk together
wearing white and blue,
dresses and pants.
Some fought to wear pants.
Some fought to wear blue,
like my child.

When you told me you might skip this day,
I knew it was time to speak plainly.
On the phone, I said the words,
My child is transgender.
The school counselor promised
a blue graduation gown
and said we would hear your chosen name
called out at the ceremony.

I asked the photographer,
a family friend, to take new photos.
Your waist-length blond hair gone,
the ruby ring back in the box.
Instead, you wore an enamel pin of a hummingbird,

a creature who defends its territory.

You are still emerging,
even now.
And in every instar
I sit wide-eyed and amazed.
This person who was once
only a sense of communion within me
is now the peak of my strength.

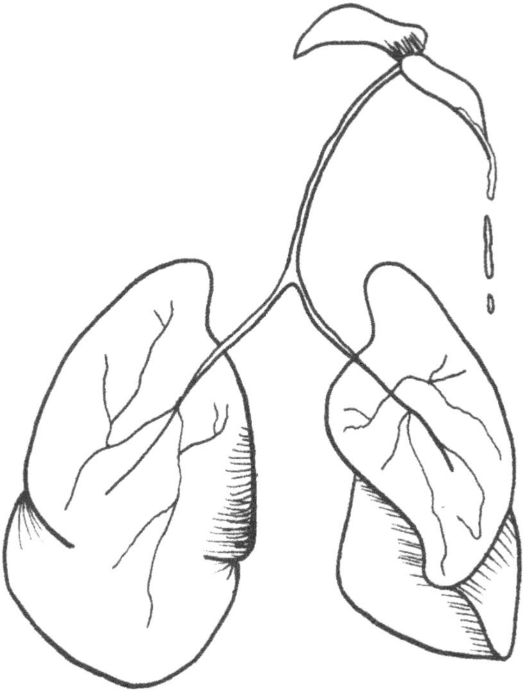

MINDFULNESS WORKAROUNDS

(Tonight, the teacher said, *ground yourselves with earth and sky*)

If the earth is hidden under cold cement,
feel the gravity that keeps your feet on the floor.

If the sky is hidden from view,
marvel at the air that flows in and out of your lungs.

If no benevolent presence fills your mind,
think of the hands that made your chair, your food, your shirt.

The love that keeps tired hands working is also there for you.

You are not alone.
You are All One.

May you be peaceful and at ease.
May all beings around you be peaceful and at ease.
May peace and ease be All.

THE SOUND OF PAPER

my eyes are itchy and heavy
yet I still pick up the pen
soothed as it drags across the paper
the silky scratching out of what I want to say
I'll do it over and over
until I learn to speak from the chest

CONSTRICTION

In a city of 30,000 people,
we eat dinner alone, overhearing the chefs.
You should go and get a haircut,
says one to the other. *I like to have a woman touch my head.*
The waiter brings me a drink that is kitchen-cleanser yellow,
yours is rose orange.
The elderly gentleman at the table near the window
is ordering his third salad.
His wife leaves the table and walks to the ladies room.
She's bent over almost in half.
I remember my grandfather walked that way,
close to the end.
How much of his end will be my end too?
When she returns,
I hear her ask the server for a glass of water.
She says, *Thank you,*
but flicks her wrist to shoo him away,

like an angry queen.
I never want to be that queen
or live that long with pain.

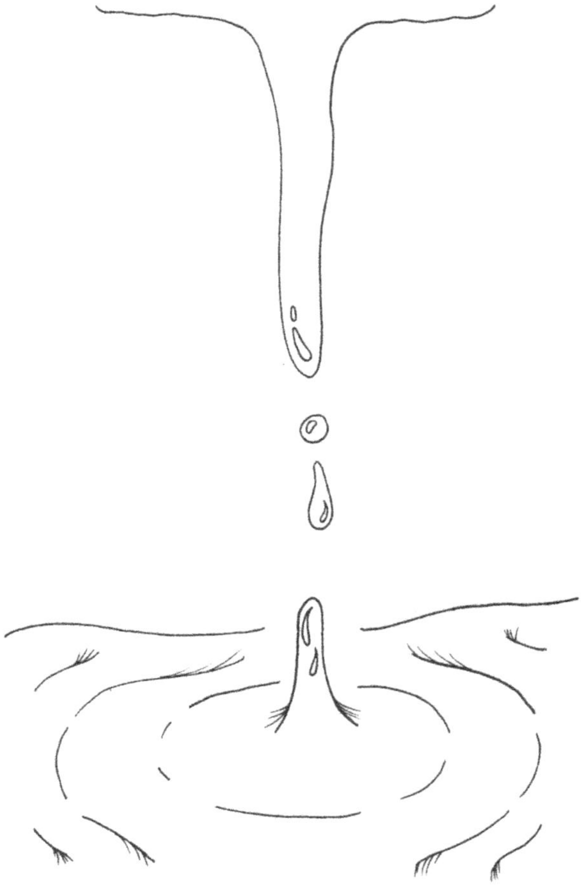

GRASPING

I want something to be good at.
I want something.
I want to be good.
I want to be.
I want.

Want is like this.
It feels like water
running over the heart.

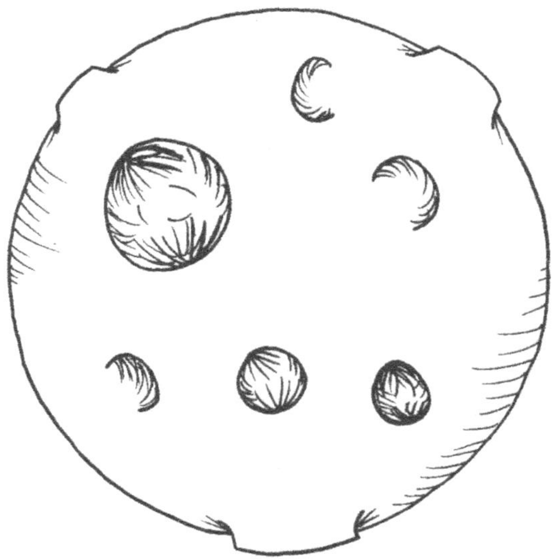

WANING ATTENTION

Every time I look
the moon has a different face.
She's not waiting
for my attention.
Hurry up,
she says,
like a mother holding car keys.

I'm taking too long with my shoelaces,
watching moths chase each other,
wondering how I got that bruise on my shin.

And she's already moving,
looking away,
not hearing me say,
I'm coming,
as I trip and fall,
hands slapping down
on the hard ground.
I'm standing back up
mind clear, hands dirty, flesh stinging.

Always I'm pulled back down to this body
while the moon
pulls oceans but can't hold
my attention.
Her face is a bright glint,
a high cheekbone
turning away from my fickle affection.
If you loved me, you'd understand me better,
she could say.

I understand little and love much.
Though I know,
she'll soon leave me in darkness,
my heart will beat fast to see her again.
Is it love?
Or admiration?
I only have the rest of my life
to find out.

APPRECIATION

I'm sitting on the oak that fell two summers ago,
and first cat jumps up to greet me.
Second cat is mewing and crunching
through the leaves behind us.

I call to her,
but she wants first cat's attention,
and walks to her instead.

A smooth, rolling sound,
and you open and shut the back sliding door.
You're walking to the other garage,
your steps echoing across the flagstone.

First cat's ears turn forward,
her chin up, then down, as she leaps off the log.
She trots away to follow you,
second cat running after,
leaves tossed in their wake.

I'm left behind as love's witness,
appreciating your charisma from afar,

like the time I found our son's school essay
where he wrote, *my dad is my hero.*
Or the time I found your shirts
in our daughter's laundry.

Or even the time I stayed in the audience
while you played guitar
at the Queen, in Wilmington,
and all those people cheered for you.
Your body rolled with the beat,
and no worry could touch you.

ACKNOWLEDGMENTS

I write in a home studio I call Kalmia Hill, after the *Kalmia latifolia* that grows here and where I'm surrounded by the life of the eastern woodlands. My first wish is to thank the life that's here, endlessly unfolding and stirring my imagination.

Thank you to my husband, Bobby Doney, who shared my vision of a house in the woods. You took my hand on the mossy path our first time here, and I knew we were home. When I was still afraid of spiders, you cleared a trail through the woods and walked me through, leading the way. Sometimes love means being brave when both of us are scared, and I can always count on your bravery.

Thank you to Kristen Lewis, our realtor, who listened and found this place for us.

Thank you to my art professor, Mark Donohue, who reminded me all trees are not the same and taught me to look closer.

Thank you to Patti Paulus of the Palette and the Page and champion of the arts here in Cecil County, for connecting me to Michelle Rothwell. Michelle, thank you for Holistic Creativity and telling me about "the dream behind the dream". Thank you to Meredith Boas of Grunge Muffin Designs for your confidence in me and for connecting me to Jodi Jackola of Tivshe Publishing. Jodi, thank you for taking a chance on a poet.

Thank you to Maggie Queenie of the Poetry Foundation for your Forms and Features workshops and the safe, creative, space you held for me. Thank you to Lisa Lutwyche, for your warmth and generous instruction in the Newark Free Library writing workshops. Thank you to studiochastain for reviewing the manuscript and providing editorial notes.

Thank you to the Insight Meditation Society of Greater Washington and the Mindful Dialogue group, led by Michael Cohen, who often reads us a poem as we close and inspired me to keep trying to put words to my feelings. Thank you to my wise friends at the Cecil County Recovery Sangha, Buddha Thunk, and Empty Circle Meditation for teaching me about sangha and speaking up.

Thank you to my parents, Gina and Dave, who convinced me reading was worth the trouble and then made sure I always had books. Thank you to my father-in-law, Bob, for your steady support over the years and the way you show us how to do hard things. Thank you to all my extended family who've encouraged my creativity over the years.

Thank you to my friends who walked the path of motherhood with me: Maia, Valerie, Julia, and Blythe, thanks for being my circle of support.

Thank you to all the creative and kind people I've met in the virtual world and the words of encouragement and appreciation that remind me I belong.

Thank you to my son, Gray, for gardening with me, and allowing me to convince you that spiders are cool. Thank you to my daughter, Cora, for giving me a book of poetry prompts and believing I could fill it. Both of you helped me grow up and love more. Thank you for connecting me to all of life.

ABOUT THE AUTHOR

Stacy Doney is a poet, artist, and a lifelong journal writer. As a child, she lived in New York, Massachusetts, and Virginia, before settling in Cecil County, Maryland with her husband to raise their two children. In every place she's lived or visited, it's been the outdoors that has inspired her most. In 2014, she and her family moved to a house in the woods where she enjoys studying nature up close. These moments of wonder often show up in her writing.